·INNOVATORS·

Tim Burton

Filmmaker

Other titles in the Innovators series include:

INNOVATORS

Tim Burton
Filmmaker

RACHEL LYNETTE

KIDHAVEN PRESS

An imprint of Thomson Gale, a part of The Thomson Corporation

THOMSON

™

GALE

Detroit • New York • San Francisco • San Diego • New Haven, Conn. • Waterville, Maine • London • Munich

LIBRARY OF CONGRESS CATALOGING-IN-PUBLICATION DATA

Lynette, Rachel.
  Tim Burton, filmmaker / by Rachel Lynette.
    p. cm. — (Innovators)
  Includes bibliographical references and index.
  ISBN 0-7377-3556-2 (alk. paper)
  1. Burton, Tim, 1958—Juvenile literature. 2. Motion picture producers and directors—United States—Biography—Juvenile literature. I. Title. II. Series.
  PN1998.3.B875L96 2006
  791.4302'33092—dc22

                                               2006002044

CONTENTS

CHAPTER 1

A Dark Beginning

Tim Burton is one of the most original and imaginative film-makers of his generation. His movies are usually dark and haunting, sometimes funny, and often touching. They frequently have an element of fantasy and horror. From the 1985 hit *Pee-Wee's Big Adventure* to the more recent *The Corpse Bride*, almost all of Burton's movies feature characters and situations that could not actually happen in real life. Burton is also known for using lighting, **sets**, and music to create a feeling of gloom and sadness. His main characters are often outcasts and misunderstood outsiders who cannot seem to fit into normal society. Burton's ability to make the fantastic believable and bring his characters to life in a way that touches his audiences is a main reason for his success.

Although Burton is also a **producer** of movies and has also written movie scripts, he is best known as a **director**. A director's job is to take a **screenplay**, or script, and make it into a movie. The director is in charge of almost every aspect of the movie. He or she works with actors, writers, set designers, the lighting crew,

Tim Burton hams it up with a spider. Like the photo,
his movies are both humorous and haunting.

makeup and wardrobe artists, and scores of other people. In many ways, the success of the movie depends on the director.

Burton has worked on over a dozen movies. Most have done well and made money for the studios that produced them. A few have been blockbuster hits. The first *Batman* movie, for example, cost $35 million to make, but earned over $400 million. *Charlie and the Chocolate Factory*, which was released in 2005, made over $450 million. Burton is surprised by his own success. He never expected to be a famous director. Like so many of his characters, Burton has always felt like an outsider.

Burton, like Charlie Bucket in *Charlie and the Chocolate Factory*, often felt like an outsider.

A Lonely Child

Timothy William Burton was born on August 25, 1958, in Burbank, California. His father, Bill, was a former minor league baseball player who worked for the Burbank Parks and Recreation Department. His mother, Jean, owned a gift shop called Cats Plus, which sold cat-related items. Tim's younger brother, Daniel, was born in 1961.

Although he grew up in a typical American family in a typical American **suburb,** Tim did not have a happy childhood. He recalls that he was a sad child who kept to himself. He did not even feel close to his family. His father wanted him to play sports and his mother tried to get him interested in playing the clarinet, but Tim resisted both. He spent a great deal of his time in his room or watching TV.

When he was ten years old, Tim went to live with his grandmother. She allowed him to spend even more time by himself, which he appreciated. He did not have many friends. Unlike other kids his age, he was not interested in after-school activities, sports, or popular music. He felt like he did not fit in, especially at school, where he was not a good student.

Although he felt alone in his world, Tim did find one thing that made him feel at home: monster movies. He spent many hours watching these movies on TV and in theaters. He identified with Frankenstein, Godzilla, and the Creature from the Black Lagoon. Tim felt that the creatures in the movies were not evil; rather, they were just misunderstood. In his mind, it was the people trying to destroy the creatures who were the real monsters. In the book *Burton on Burton*, he says, "I've always loved monsters and monster movies. I was never terrified of them, I just loved them from as early as I can remember. . . . I

Super 8mm Cameras

As a teenager, Burton made his first movies using a Super 8mm camera. At that time video camcorders had not yet been invented, so people used 8mm cameras to make home movies. These were usually in black and white and had no sound.

The Super 8mm camera, which was put on the market in 1965, got its name from the film it used, which was 8 mm (0.31m) wide. The film came in spools 50 feet (15.2m) long, which was enough to film for three minutes and twenty seconds. The cameras were set to film at eighteen frames per second, which resulted in a movie with a flickering, choppy appearance.

Although most people today use camcorders to make home movies, some people who like the look of the 8mm movies continue to use the cameras. The only company that still makes 8mm cameras is located in Russia, but people can buy used ones from secondhand stores and online auction sites.

As a youth, Tim Burton spent many hours watching monster movies like *Frankenstein*.

felt the monsters were basically misperceived, they usually had much more heartfelt souls than the human characters around them."[1] Burton especially admired the work of Vincent Price, a popular actor who starred in many horror movies in the 1950s and '60s.

Early Creations

Tim did not just watch monster movies; he also made them. Thirteen-year-old Tim and a small group of friends used a black-and-white Super 8mm camera to shoot several short films. One was about a werewolf and another, called *The Island of Doctor Agor*, was about a mad scientist. A third showed a

Burton, who has been making movies since age thirteen, watches over the filming of one of his movies.

beanbag chair attacking Tim in his sleep. He had no idea then that he would someday direct blockbuster movies. In fact, he wanted to be an artist.

Tim spent a great deal of time drawing. Most of his pictures were quite elaborate. He liked to draw monsters and aliens fighting each other or battling armies in complicated war scenes. Although he did not take any drawing classes, his talent was noticed by people in his community. When Tim was in the ninth grade he won first prize in a contest to create an antilittering poster. The prize was $10, and his winning poster was displayed on all the garbage trucks in Burbank. Tim also earned extra money painting holiday pictures on his neighbors' windows for Halloween and Christmas.

Learning Animation

When Tim Burton turned eighteen, his artistic talent won him a scholarship to the California Institute of the Arts (Cal Arts) in Valencia, California, to study **animation**. Animation is a technique in which many pictures that are only slightly different from **frame** to frame are filmed. When the pictures are shown at a rapid rate, it appears as though the characters and objects in them are moving. Burton thought that working in animation would be a good way for him to earn a living because it combined two of his passions: drawing and moviemaking.

Burton enjoyed his time at Cal Arts. For the first time in his life he was among other people who shared his interests, and he was free to use his imagination and to further develop his own drawing style. He used his own ideas to create the characters he animated. He designed and drew the backgrounds for the characters. He learned to represent his ideas using a **storyboard**, a

Monster Movies of the 1950s

Godzilla, the Blob, the Creature from the Black Lagoon, and the dozens of other monsters that Burton loved as a child were all part of what has often been called the "monster movie" decade. During the 1950s monster movies flourished in theaters and on TV. Some people think that these movies were popular because they reflected the fears about atomic weapons and about the threat of communism that arose after World War II. This may be especially true of movies about aliens. The aliens' attempts to take over the world in these movies can be compared to the communists, who Americans feared had a similar goal.

Most of these films had small budgets and featured lesser-known actors, predictable plot lines, and inexpensive special effects. For example, the monsters were often played by actors dressed in rubber costumes. At one point in his childhood, Burton's career goal was to become the actor who wore Godzilla's rubber costume.

An actor is helped into a costume during the filming of Creature from the Black Lagoon.

sequence of pictures used to show different shots for a film. Burton later told *Rolling Stone* reporter David Breskin, "What I feel really good about, really happy about, is that I did not go to film school. I went to Cal Arts, and went through animation where I got a very solid education."[2]

Each year, the school had a competition. The students made short animated movies and people from Disney Studios watched them. The students who made the movies that the Disney people thought were the best were hired as animators. In his third year at Cal Arts, Burton made a movie called *The Stalk of the Celery Monster*. This movie won him a job at Disney Studios as an **apprentice** animator. Burton's childhood fascination with monster movies and love of drawing had led him to a budding career.

CHAPTER 2

Finding His Own Path

Burton started work at Disney Studios in 1979 as an animator for the movie *The Fox and the Hound*. He describes this time as the most depressing period of his life. He hated drawing the same things over and over and not being able to use his own creative ideas and unique drawing style. He was not even good at it. According to Burton, "I got all the cute fox scenes to draw and . . . I just couldn't do it. I couldn't even fake the Disney style. Mine looked like roadkills."[3]

The people at Disney realized that *The Fox and the Hound* was not the right job for Burton and had him work instead as a **conceptual artist** on *The Black Cauldron*. As a conceptual artist, Burton was to come up with ideas for the film. Instead of copying someone else's work over and over again as he did for *The Fox and the Hound*, Burton got to create the characters and the world in which they lived. But his ideas were not what Disney was looking for, and in the end the studio did not use any of Burton's drawings for the movie.

Vincent

Burton's talent, however, did not go unnoticed. In 1982 Disney allowed him to do his own project: a short film called *Vincent*. *Vincent* was based on a poem Burton had written for children. He decided to make it into a six-minute, **stop-motion** short film.

Tim Burton began working as an animator for Disney Studios in 1979.

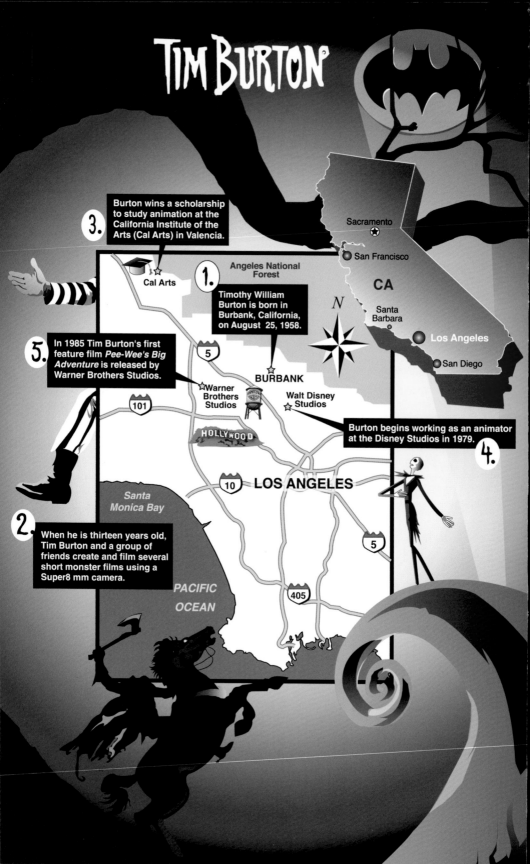

TIM BURTON

3. Burton wins a scholarship to study animation at the California Institute of the Arts (Cal Arts) in Valencia.

☆ Cal Arts

1. Angeles National Forest

Timothy William Burton is born in Burbank, California, on August 25, 1958.

Sacramento ✪

● San Francisco

CA

Santa Barbara ●

● Los Angeles

● San Diego

N

5. In 1985 Tim Burton's first feature film *Pee-Wee's Big Adventure* is released by Warner Brothers Studios.

5

101

☆ Warner Brothers Studios

Walt Disney ☆ Studios

BURBANK

HOLLYWOOD

Burton begins working as an animator at the Disney Studios in 1979. **4.**

10 **LOS ANGELES**

Santa Monica Bay

5

2. When he is thirteen years old, Tim Burton and a group of friends create and film several short monster films using a Super8 mm camera.

405

PACIFIC OCEAN

Stop-motion animation is made by setting up a scene with puppets and filming just one **frame**. Then the puppets are moved a small amount and another frame is shot. The frames are shown at a rate of twenty-four per second, making it appear as if the puppets are moving. Thousands of frames must be shot to make even a short movie.

The main character in *Vincent* is a seven-year-old boy who dreams of being just like Vincent Price. He imagines dipping his aunt in hot wax and making his dog into a zombie. But his mother brings him back to reality, saying, "You are not Vincent Price, you're Vincent Malloy/You're not tormented or insane, you're just a young boy."[4]

Burton both wrote and directed the film, which was shot in black and white. The puppets were modeled after drawings he created. Not surprisingly, the Vincent puppet looked a lot like Burton himself.

Burton wanted the real Vincent Price to narrate the film. He sent Price the storyboards for the movie along with his request. Burton was nervous about writing to his childhood idol and worried that Price would not like his work. But Price loved the film and agreed to do the narration. He and Burton began a friendship that lasted until Price's death in 1993.

Although Disney executives were pleased with *Vincent*, they did not see much market value in the short, dark film. It was not widely released, but it did show at several film festivals, and won the praise of critics as well as two awards. It also led to Burton's next directing project: *Frankenweenie*.

Frankenweenie

Frankenweenie was a twenty-five-minute-long film loosely based on the 1931 movie *Frankenstein*. Like *Vincent*, *Frankenweenie* was

Vincent Price

By the time Burton met Vincent Price in 1982, Price was 71 years old and had acted in nearly one hundred films. Many of these were the low-budget horror movies for which he is most remembered. Two of his best-known movies were *The House of Wax* (1954) and *House of Usher* (1960).

The House of Wax is about a sculptor (played by Price) who opens a wax museum with a gruesome secret. The sculptures are not made entirely of wax but are instead the bodies of dead people that have

only been covered with a layer of wax. *House of Usher* was the first in a series of movies based on the stories of Edgar Allan Poe. Burton loved these movies as a child and some critics believe they influenced his directing style as an adult.

Price's final film role was as the inventor in Burton's *Edward Scissorhands*. Burton also produced a tribute to Price that aired on television shortly after the actor's death in 1993.

Vincent Price acted in nearly one hundred films.

shot in black and white, but this time Burton used real people, including well-known actors Shelley Duvall and Daniel Stern. Although he did not actually write the script, the film was based on some of Burton's drawings and his own feelings about living in the suburbs.

The story is about a boy named Victor Frankenstein who uses electricity to bring his beloved dog, Sparky, back to life after the animal is run over by a car. Although Sparky looks a bit odd—he has clearly been sewn back together and he has bolts in his neck—he is still the same lovable pet he used to be. Unfortunately, the neighbors do not approve. They try to kill Sparky and in the process nearly kill Victor. The final scenes of the movie feature an angry mob, a raging fire, a heroic rescue, and eventually a happy ending.

Frankenweenie was intended to be shown with the rerelease of *Pinocchio* in 1984. However, it received a PG rating and therefore could not be shown with a G-rated film. Burton was shocked at the rating because he felt that his film was much less violent and disturbing than *Pinocchio*.

Pee-Wee Goes to the Movies

Although *Frankenweenie* was not released to the public, it was shown in private screenings. Comedian Paul Reubens was at one of these screenings. When he saw the film, Reubens knew that Burton was the perfect person to bring his character, Pee-Wee Herman, to the big screen.

Burton was twenty-six when he met Reubens. By then, Reubens's character of Pee-Wee Herman was well developed. Pee-Wee Herman was a grown man, but his bizarre and often immature behavior made him seem more like a spoiled child. He always dressed in a gray suit with a red bow tie. He had a large collection of toys, including his most prized possession: a shiny red bicycle.

In His Own World

Burton was thrilled when a representative from Warner Brothers Studios asked him to direct the movie *Pee-Wee's Big Adventure*. He liked the material and he needed another project since he had quit his job at Disney after finishing *Frankenweenie*. He also felt that he understood the Pee-Wee Herman character. According to Burton, "The Pee-Wee character was just into what he was doing . . . it was nice that he didn't really care about how he was perceived. He operated in his own world and there's something I find very admirable about that."[5]

In the movie, Pee-Wee's beloved bicycle is stolen. He goes on a cross-country trek to get it back, and on the way meets many interesting characters. Burton was careful to not put too many of his own ideas into the film. He understood that although he was the director, it was really Reubens's movie. But Burton was still able to add some of his own personal touches. For example, there are two parts that feature stop-motion animation. Burton used this technique to animate a scene in which Pee-Wee dreams his bicycle is being eaten by a tyrannosaurus rex. He also used stop motion to animate a truck driver named Large Marge. Many people think that Large Marge's distorting head is one of the funniest parts of the movie.

Another way that Burton enhanced the movie was with his unexpected choice of composer for the musical **score**. Burton hired Danny Elfman, lead singer of the pop band Oingo Boingo, to create music for the movie. Although Elfman had never scored a movie before, the circus-like music he wrote turned out to be perfect for *Pee-Wee's Big Adventure*. The film was the first of many that Elfman would score for Burton.

Pee-Wee Herman, played by actor Paul Reubens,
was the star of Burton's first feature film.

Pee-Wee Herman and his prized bicycle swing in a scene from *Pee-Wee's Big Adventure*.

Although the movie did well at the box office, making over $40 million for Warner Brothers, it was not praised by most critics. *Pee-Wee's Big Adventure* got more than its share of bad reviews. It even made several "Worst Films of 1985" lists. The bad reviews were upsetting to Burton, who had never been on the receiving end of so much negative criticism before. But despite the reviews, Burton was satisfied with the work he had done and glad that the film had made money for the studio.

Danny Elfman, lead singer for Oingo Boingo, wrote music for several of Burton's films including *Pee-Wee's Big Adventure.*

Bad Reviews for *Pee-Wee*

Burton's first feature-length film, *Pee-Wee's Big Adventure*, was hailed as comic genius by some critics, but many others found it to be boring, stupid, and pointless. *New York Times* film critic Vincent Canby described it as "the most barren comedy I have seen in years, maybe ever." Critic Bill Hagen of the *San Diego Union-Tribune* went even further, comparing the film to a root canal, a painful dental procedure, and advising people to avoid it if at all possible.

More recent reviews have been kinder to the film. Many of these were written by reviewers who first saw the movie when they were children. Their fond memories of the film may be why they have a more positive viewpoint than other critics.

Vincent Canby, "Screen: *Pee-Wee's Big Adventure*, a Comedy." *The New York Times*, August 9, 1985.

Although his start at Disney was a difficult one, Burton had not given up. His projects were getting bigger and bigger, and he was starting to earn a reputation as an original and creative director.

CHAPTER 3

Misfits and Outcasts

Burton's box office success with *Pee-Wee's Big Adventure* made him a sought-after director. Over the next few years he looked at numerous scripts but did not find any that he wanted to direct until he saw the script for *Beetlejuice*. Burton was drawn to the project because of its imaginative plot and because it was both a horror movie and a comedy. It also required elaborate, spooky sets and many special effects, both of which appealed to Burton.

The movie is about a couple who become ghosts after they are killed in a car accident. When a family they do not like moves into their old house, the couple tries to scare them away. Their efforts are not successful, so they seek the help of another ghost, named Betelgeuse.

While Burton was working on *Beetlejuice,* executives at Warner Brothers approached him about directing *Batman*. Based on the original *Batman* comics, the movie is about billionaire Bruce Wayne. Wayne lives in crime-ridden Gotham City and is haunted by the murder of his parents when he was a child. In an effort to

Burton's second feature film starred actor Michael
Keaton as a ghost named *Betelgeuse.*

avenge his parents, he develops the secret identity of Batman. As
Batman, Wayne fights The Joker, an insane criminal who plans to
take over Gotham City.

Burton's Dark Side

One of the reasons that Burton wanted to direct *Batman* was that
he felt that he understood the Batman character. He says, "I loved

Batman, the split personality, the hidden person. It's a character I could relate to. Having those two sides, a light side and a dark one and not being able to resolve them."[6] It is important to Burton to connect to the characters he directs. Many observers believe this is why he tends to do movies about dark characters, who, like himself, have trouble fitting in with the people around them.

Even though he is a well-known director, Burton often feels like an outsider. He has suffered frequent bouts of depression and has a reputation for being short-tempered and moody. In his twenties he had a hard time communicating with people and

Burton poses with the Batmobile while working on *Batman*.

rarely made eye contact. Burton usually prefers to be alone rather than with other people. Even his appearance is unusual—he has pale skin, droopy eyes, and an unruly mop of dark hair. He dresses only in black.

Despite his reputation, Burton does have a few close friends. He has also had three long-term relationships. The first was with German artist Lena Gieseke, whom he met while filming *Batman*. The two were married in 1989.

Batman

During the first year of his marriage to Gieseke, Burton worked on *Batman*, a much bigger movie than anything he had worked on before. The production budget for *Beetlejuice* was $15 million. For Batman, it was $40 million. Burton filmed the movie at Pinewood Studios in Great Britain, where his sets took up most of the 95-acre (30ha) backlot and seventeen **soundstages**.

Burton faced several challenges working on *Batman*. One of the first problems he encountered was resistance to his choice for the lead role. Burton cast Michael Keaton as the star of his movie. Many people doubted that Keaton would make a good Batman. He did not have a muscular build and was not considered to be an action-adventure actor. Angry fans wrote hundreds of letters to Warner Brothers demanding that the part be recast. But Burton stood by his decision. He told interviewer Alan Jones, "I looked at actors that were more the fan image of Batman, but I felt it was such an uninteresting way to go."[7]

Another challenge Burton faced was that the writers kept rewriting parts of the script during filming. The writers got new ideas or realized that certain parts of the script would not work as well as they had originally thought. The constant changes were confusing and frustrating for Burton. He struggled to make the

Burton cast Michael Keaton as the dark
hero Batman.

The Original Batman

Tim Burton's *Batman* movie was based on the original Batman character created by Bob Kane, a twenty-two-year-old illustrator for DC Comics, in May 1939. Kane's assignment was to create a superhero as appealing as Superman, who had been created the year before. Kane had three inspirations for his creation. These were a sketch by artist Leonardo da Vinci of a man with wings like a bat's; a silent movie called *The Bat Whisperer,* about a man with the face of a bat; and images of the legendary masked hero Zorro.

Batman was different from other superheroes because he did not have any super powers. Rather, he relied on his superior training, intellect, and a host of high-tech tools and weapons. The best known of these were the Batmobile and the Bat Utility Belt, which seemed to contain exactly what the superhero needed in every situation.

Batman gained immediate popularity with readers, who were intrigued with his dark personality and host of outrageous enemies including The Joker, The Penguin, The Riddler, and Catwoman. Burton, too, loved these villains, all of whom appear in the two Batman movies he directed.

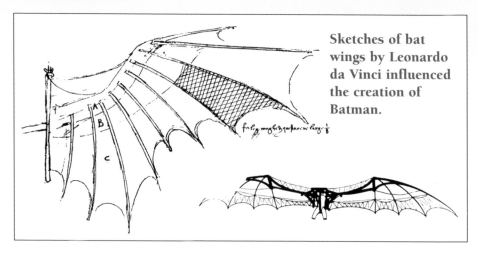

Sketches of bat wings by Leonardo da Vinci influenced the creation of Batman.

movie flow smoothly and to be sure that the plot was not too hard to follow. He told Jones, "It was tough from the point of having no time to regroup after the script revisions; I never had time to think about them. I always felt like I was catching up."[8]

Burton also felt the pressure of working on a big-budget picture. Studio executives had high hopes for the film. They had put a lot of money into it and expected it to make a lot of money back for them. In addition, millions of Batman fans were waiting to see how Burton would portray the beloved comic book character. This was also the first time that Burton had worked with a major star. Jack Nicholson, who played The Joker, was a superstar in Hollywood.

Burton met these challenges, and when *Batman* came out in 1989 it was a huge success. Most of the fans liked the darker Batman that Burton created. However, Burton himself was not happy with the film. He felt that he let the script unravel, which resulted in a confusing plot with holes and inconsistencies. Burton eventually agreed to make the sequel, *Batman Returns*, because he wanted to correct these mistakes. But before working on the second Batman movie, Burton did a project of his own.

Edward Scissorhands

Between the two Batman movies, Burton wrote, produced, and directed *Edward Scissorhands*. The idea for the movie came from one of his many drawings. Burton drew constantly, both on and off the set. The drawing that inspired the movie was of a young man who had large, razor-sharp scissors instead of hands.

In the movie, which has been described as a modern-day fairy tale, Edward is the creation of an inventor (played by Vincent Price), who died before he could give Edward hands. An unusually shy and gentle man, Edward is left to go through life unable to touch anyone without hurting them. He is taken in by

Johnny Depp played the strange character of Edward Scissorhands. Depp also appeared in several other Burton films.

a kind woman and for a while is welcomed by her neighbors, who are thrilled with his ability to sculpt shrubs and cut hair. But affection soon turns to fear. There is a violent confrontation, after which Edward is exiled from the suburbs.

Burton cast Johnny Depp to play the part of Edward. Burton felt that Depp had an innocent quality that was key to Edward's character. He also thought that Depp had expressive eyes, which was important because the character does not speak very much. Burton and Depp worked well together and went on to become good friends.

Johnny Depp's Big Break

When Johnny Depp first read the script for Burton's *Edward Scissorhands,* he was the teen-idol star of *21 Jump Street,* a TV show about cops who pose as high school students. Depp felt trapped in the role and was eager to move on. He felt that he identified with Edward's loneliness, freakishness, and need to be loved.

To prepare for a meeting with Burton to discuss the movie, Depp read children's stories, fairy tales, and child psychology books. He watched all of Burton's movies and read as much as he could about the director.

The meeting went smoothly, but Depp still felt he had only a slim chance of getting the part because other much more experienced actors were also being considered.

Depp was ecstatic weeks later when he got the call telling him the part was his. Depp credits Burton with the majority of his success as an actor, saying, "Because of Tim's belief in me, Hollywood opened its doors, playing a strange follow-the-leader game."

Quoted in Mark Salisbury, *Burton on Burton.* London: Faber and Faber, 2000, pg. xii.

Johnny Depp felt he identified with the Edward Scissorhands character.

Though not a blockbuster, the movie did well. Most of the reviews from critics were positive, praising Burton's imaginative style. Many reviewers also noted that the movie was obviously a very personal one for Burton. In it, Burton's own feelings and life experiences are strong themes.

Like Edward, Burton felt he did not fit in with his surroundings, especially when he was young. He talks about this in an interview with Kristine McKenna: "School is your first taste of categorization . . . and you don't have to do much to be put in a weird category. I felt very lonely in school, and *Edward Scissorhands* was based on the loneliness I experienced as a kid."[9]

Burton may have felt lonely as a child, but by the time *Edward Scissorhands* was released, he was very much in demand. With four successful major motion pictures to his credit, Burton was one of the hottest directors in Hollywood.

CHAPTER 4

Branching Out

Soon after *Edward Scissorhands* was released in 1990, Burton began working on *Batman Returns*. Although the movie did very well at the box office, some critics felt that the character of Batman was even darker in this movie than in the first one. Burton agrees. He believes that problems he was having in his personal life influenced how he directed the movie. His marriage to Gieseke came to an end during the filming, and a close friend committed suicide. Burton was depressed and struggled more than usual to relate to other people. His reputation for being inconsiderate and difficult to work with worsened.

Burton's life improved dramatically on New Year's Eve in 1991 when he met model Lisa Marie. The two fell in love, and friends say that the relationship changed Burton's life. He became more focused and easier to work with, and even started dressing better.

During this time Burton was also working on *The Nightmare Before Christmas*. Burton had proposed this project to Disney ten years earlier. At that time Disney executives were not interested in producing the project. However, Disney still retained the **rights** to the project, and by 1991, the studio was eager to work with Burton, by then one of the most successful directors in Hollywood.

Burton produced *Nightmare*, but he did not direct it because he was still working on *Batman Returns*. He also created the characters, wrote the script, and made sure that the crew stayed focused on his vision. The movie was done using stop-motion animation, a process that took so long that only about seventy seconds of film was shot each week. As a result, the movie took three years to complete.

Tim Burton directs Michelle Pfeiffer and Michael Keaton during the filming of *Batman Returns*.

Burton produced but did not direct the stop-motion
animation film *The Nightmare Before Christmas*.

In the film, once again, Burton's main character is misunderstood by the people around him. Jack Skellington, the Pumpkin King of Halloweentown, decides that he wants to take over Christmas. But he does not quite understand the holiday. After kidnapping Santa Claus, Jack delivers strange and scary toys made by the spooky residents of Halloweentown. Children are terrified, and Jack's version of Christmas is a failure.

The movie, however, was not. Once again, Burton was praised for his originality. Although some parents thought the movie was too scary for children, Burton disagreed. He believes that children should decide for themselves if something is too scary and that adults should give them the freedom to make those choices.

Johnny Depp portrayed a filmmaker in *Ed Wood*, one of Burton's smaller successes.

After *Nightmare*, Burton made three more movies in the 1990s: *Ed Wood, Mars Attacks!* and *Sleepy Hollow.* Johnny Depp starred in two of them, and Burton's girlfriend, Lisa Marie, had small roles in all three. The movies were well received by critics and made money, but none of them were blockbuster hits.

Oyster Boy

Throughout his moviemaking career, Burton has continued to draw and write. He says that writing calms him and helps him to focus. In 1997 he published a book of twenty-three short poems called *The Melancholy Death of Oyster Boy and Other Stories.* The poems feature strange, misshapen characters, most of whom come to a bad end. Some of the characters include Mummy Boy (whose head is mistaken for a piñata); Melonhead; and Jimmy, the Hideous Penguin Boy. The book was illustrated with Burton's simple, yet spooky pictures. The most gruesome picture is of "The Boy with Nails in His Eyes." He dedicated the book to Lisa Marie, who he said inspired many of the poems.

Planet of the Apes

Burton's relationship with Lisa Marie lasted for nine years. Her last role in a Burton film was as a minor character in the 2001 big-budget movie *Planet of the Apes.*

At first, Burton was not interested in directing the movie because he did not want to remake the original *Planet of the Apes*, which was released in 1968. But studio executives told him the new film would be a "reimagining" rather than a remake. Burton felt that this gave him the freedom to put his own mark on the classic story.

Another reason Burton was drawn to the movie was that he was excited about using humans to play the apes. In an interview with

Lisa Marie in Burton's Movies

Lisa Marie had small but important roles in four of Burton's movies. The couple's first movie together was *Ed Wood*. In this film Lisa Marie plays Vampira, the host of a late-night television show that features B-grade horror movies.

Lisa Marie's role of Vampira differed from her other Burton roles in two important ways. It included much more dialogue than any of the other roles. It was also the only one in which her character did not endure a gruesome death. In *Mars Attacks!* Lisa Marie plays a bizarre-looking Martian. It took several hours each day to get her into her makeup and costume, which included a 20-

Lisa Marie played a Martian in Burton's *Mars Attacks!*

pound (10kg) hairpiece and a dress so tight it had to be sewn on. In the movie, the character meets her death when she is shot by CIA agents. In *Sleepy Hollow* Lisa Marie has a small part as the main character's mother, who is killed by her husband in an iron maiden, a coffinlike box lined with spikes. In *Planet of the Apes*, her final movie with Burton, Lisa Marie plays Nova, an ape who is killed by her own father while she is trying to protect one of the humans.

Reel.com he said, "There was only one thing I felt was important—having humans play the apes. These days you can [use computer-generated images] all the way and there is no way. The energy isn't there."[10]

Planet of the Apes is about an astronaut who accidentally lands on a planet that is ruled by talking apes. There are also humans

Burton cast human actors in the ape roles in his *Planet of the Apes*.

Ape School

Burton hired Terry Notary to teach the *Planet of the Apes* actors how to act like primates. Notary had portrayed several animals in performances for Cirque du Soleil, a circus that features only human performers. Although he was not an expert in ape behavior, he soon became one. Notary read everything he could find about apes; watched wildlife documentaries; and spent countless hours observing real chimpanzees, orangutans, and gorillas.

Ape School started at 2:00 A.M. each day because after four hours of ape training, it took another four hours to apply the elaborate makeup and costumes needed for the day's filming. The actors were instructed to "find their inner ape" as they learned how to move and behave like apes.

Actress Helena Bonham Carter, who plays the female lead in the movie, had a hard time learning the behaviors, saying that she failed Ape School. But after working one-on-one with Notary, and spending time with real chimps on the set, she was able to overcome her difficulties.

on the planet, but the apes consider them to be stupid animals, and hunt them to be used as slaves. The movie culminates in a large-scale battle scene between the humans and the apes.

To help the actors act more like apes, Burton sent them to "Ape School" for six weeks. He had the actors study real primates and hired stuntman Terry Notary to teach them how to move, eat, and even fight like apes.

Planet of the Apes did not do as well at the box office as the studio had expected, and it received mixed reviews. Many critics felt that the story was too slow and the plot contained too many holes. But most agreed that the movie was visually stunning. The ape world that Burton created is dark, filled with creeping vines and cavelike rooms. The apes that live in this world are also quite amazing, due to their elaborate costumes and makeup. Critics also praised the performance of Helena Bonham Carter, who had a starring role as an ape who tries to help the humans.

Burton was also pleased with Carter's performance. The two struck up a friendship that quickly turned romantic. Shortly after the movie came out in 2001, Burton broke up with Lisa Marie. He began dating Carter and the two were soon engaged. Despite *Planet of the Apes'* disappointing reviews, Burton remained a sought-after director. No matter what kind of reviews his movies received, the films were never boring. Burton was admired for his unique style and willingness to take chances.

CHAPTER 5

Chocolate and Corpses

Burton's relationship with Carter has continued to thrive. The two had a son, Billy Ray, who was born on October 4, 2003. The family lives in north London in two adjoining houses. Since Carter did not want to move, Burton bought the house next to hers and they remodeled the two homes to connect them. Burton and Carter do not just live together—they also work together. Burton cast Carter in his next three movies, *Big Fish*, *Charlie and the Chocolate Factory*, and *The Corpse Bride*.

Charlie and the Chocolate Factory

Roald Dahl's classic book *Charlie and the Chocolate Factory* was made into a movie over thirty years ago. Although many people loved the movie, Burton did not. He thought it was sappy. He also did not like the ways in which the movie was different from the book. He especially felt that the character of Willy Wonka was not portrayed as Dahl had written him. Burton wanted his version of the book to stick more closely to Dahl's original story.

Burton was given a budget of $150 million for the film. A lot of the money for the movie went into building the elaborate sets and creating the amazing special effects that were needed to bring Dahl's story to life. In the story, Charlie Bucket and four other children find golden tickets in Wonka chocolate bars that allow them to visit Willy Wonka's mysterious chocolate factory. During the tour of the bizarre, amazing, and sometimes scary factory, each of the children except Charlie manages to get into serious trouble.

Burton cast Johnny Depp in the important role of Willy Wonka. Like many of Burton's characters, Wonka is depicted as a strange man who has issues with his family and who does not know how to relate to other people.

One of the most incredible scenes in the movie is when Willy Wonka brings the five lucky children into the Chocolate Room.

Tim Burton and partner Helena Bonham Carter pose with toy characters from *The Corpse Bride*.

Rather than using **computer-generated images (CGI)** to create this room, Burton chose to build the entire set. The set takes up 45,000 square feet (13,716 sq m). The landscape was all made to look edible and includes nearly seventy different kinds of plants, 30-foot (9m) trees, and a chocolate river with a 70-foot (21m) "chocolatefalls." Burton explains, "We felt it was important to be in the environment and make it as textural as possible to give it as much reality as possible. . . . We spent months trying to find the right consistency to make the chocolate, to give it the weight so it didn't look like brown water."[11] Burton needed nearly 250,000 gallons of the fake chocolate to make his river. One of the challenges of working with the gooey liquid, which is called Nutrisol, was that after a couple of weeks it started to smell really awful.

It is in the Chocolate Room that the children first encounter the Oompa-Loompas, the little people who work in the factory. The Oompa-Loompas also perform four elaborate song-and-dance

Burton chose Johnny Depp for the eccentric Willy Wonka character in *Charlie and the Chocolate Factory*.

Special effects allowed Burton to use only one actor, Deep Roy, to play hundreds of Oompa-Loompas in *Charlie and the Chocolate Factory.*

numbers. Although there are hundreds of them in the movie, they were all played by only one actor—a 4-foot (1.2m) dwarf named Deep Roy. Burton used several kinds of special effects to multiply the Oompa-Loompas. **Remote-controlled** robots were used when the Oompa-Loompas were shot at a distance and when they did not need to do anything too complicated. Burton also used camera tricks to multiply Roy's image. For these scenes, Roy was filmed hundreds of times from many different angles. In addition, Burton used CGI for some of the trickier Oompa-Loompa scenes.

Some of the same special effects were used in the scene in which forty squirrels shell walnuts and attack one of the children. Although some of the squirrels were robots or CGIs, most of them were real. Burton had them trained to sit on stools, crack nuts, and put the nuts on a conveyor belt. It took four months to train the squirrels because these animals are very difficult to work with. To learn the behavior, each squirrel had to repeat it about two thousand times. Although the scene was difficult and expensive to film, Burton was pleased with the result.

Charlie and the Chocolate Factory was well received by audiences both young and old. People loved the spectacular world of the chocolate factory that Burton created, as well as the interesting characters.

While they were working on *Charlie*, Burton, Carter, and Depp were also working on *The Corpse Bride*. Burton was codirecting the film and Carter and Depp were doing the voices for the two main characters. They filmed *Charlie* during the day and then went to another studio to work on *The Corpse Bride* at night.

The Corpse Bride

The Corpse Bride is loosely based on a nineteenth-century Russian folktale. In the movie, the main character, a quiet, shy man named Victor, accidentally weds himself to a corpse. The corpse bride, though dead, is still beautiful and her underground world of the dead is more colorful and lively than the dark and drab world of the living.

Burton chose to film the movie using stop-motion animation. Digital technology has made this kind of animation smoother and faster than it was when Burton made *The Nightmare Before Christmas*. But it is still much slower than using CGI. Burton considered using CGI to make the movie, but it was important to him to work with real puppets and sets. He told *Editors Guild Magazine*, "Our Corpse Bride puppets are beautifully made and our animators are amazing. There's something wonderful about being able to physically touch and move the characters, and to see their world actually exist."[12]

Willy Wonka & the Chocolate Factory

Willy Wonka & the Chocolate Factory was released in 1971. Although the movie was not an immediate box office hit, over the next thirty years it grew in popularity, eventually becoming a children's classic. Much of the movie's success can be credited to actor Gene Wilder, who portrayed Willy Wonka with a gentle humor that enthralled both children and adults. Another reason for the 1971 version's enduring popularity is that it is a musical. Although Burton's version includes four songs performed by the Oompa-Loompas, the original movie included many other songs as well.

Although most viewers enjoyed *Willy Wonka & the Chocolate Factory*, one person who did not was Roald Dahl, the author of the book on which the movie was based. He felt that the movie strayed too far from his story, and he refused to sell the movie rights to the sequel, *Charlie and the Great Glass Elevator.* Dahl died in 1990. His widow, who collaborated with the writers of Burton's *Charlie and the Chocolate Factory,* says that her late husband would have approved of Burton's version.

Gene Wilder (center) poses with the original cast of Oompa-Loompas.

Burton used stop-motion filming techniques to make the characters in *The Corpse Bride* come alive.

Burton found creating the human characters to be a unique challenge because he did not want them to look exactly like real people. He looked back at his first stop-motion film, *Vincent*, for inspiration and used a similar style to design the puppets for *Corpse Bride*. In an interview with *Cinema Confidential*, Burton said, "A lot of times in stop motion, they try to do human characters that are too semi-realistic. Something's always kind of odd. I went back to the first short film I did, "Vincent," and thought about Victor who is kind of Vincent grown up."[13]

Burton also did not want his characters, especially the dead ones, to look too serious. Despite being dead, most of these characters are happy. For inspiration, Burton used images from Mexico's Day of the Dead celebrations. The Day of the Dead is a festive holiday in which the dead are honored. Images of skeletons are a big part of the celebration. Burton has many of these images around his home and has always found them intriguing.

Future Plans

The Corpse Bride was Burton's thirteenth major motion picture. Critics agree that it and his other recent movies have not been as dark as most of the other films he has done. People have speculated that his new lighter touch may be due to the fact that he is now a father. Burton disputes this, however. He told Mark Salisbury, an interviewer for the Web site *Time Out London*, "I don't foresee [fatherhood] changing in any way, shape or form the kind

Tim Burton is one of the most creative filmmakers working today, and his career is far from over.

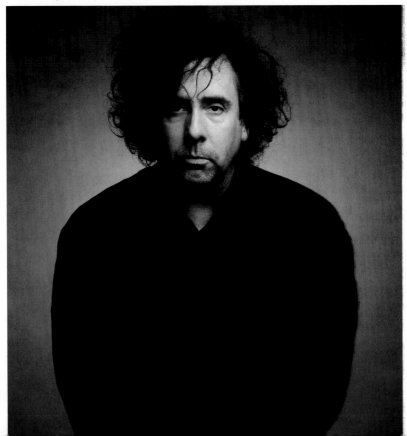

of movies I wanna make. In fact, they might get more harsh in some ways."[14]

Burton's future plans include a movie with actor Jim Carrey called *Believe It or Not!* The movie is based on the life of Robert Ripley, who spent the 1930s and '40s searching the world for amazing facts, feats, and people to write about in his popular newspaper column of the same name. *Believe It or Not!* will be filmed in London.

For over twenty years Tim Burton has used his unique vision and creativity to make movies that bring a host of strange and dark characters onto the big screen. Yet his career is far from over. Burton fans can look forward to many more creative movies from the eccentric director.

Notes

Chapter 1: A Dark Beginning

1. Quoted in Mark Salisbury, *Burton on Burton*. London: Faber and Faber, 2000, p. 2.
2. Quoted in David Breskin, *Inner Views: Filmmakers in Conversation,* New York: Da Capo Press, 1997. p. 335.

Chapter 2: Finding His Own Path

3. Quoted in Mark Salisbury, *Burton on Burton*. London: Faber and Faber, 2000, p. 9.
4. Tim Burton, *Vincent*. Walt Disney Studios, 1982.
5. Quoted in Mark Salisbury, *Burton on Burton*. London: Faber and Faber, 2000, p. 44.

Chapter 3: Misfits and Outcasts

6. Quoted in Mark Salisbury, *Burton on Burton*. London: Faber and Faber, 2000, p. 72
7. Quoted in Alan Jones, *Cinefantastique,* November 1989. www. batmanmovieonline.com/behindthescenes/articles/jokemakeup htm.
8. Quoted in Alan Jones, *Cinefantastique,* November 1989. www. batmanmovieonline.com/behindthescenes/articles/jokemakeup htm.
9. Quoted in Kristian Fraga, *Tim Burton Interviews,* Jackson University Press of Mississippi, 2005, p. 175.

Chapter 4: Branching Out

10. Quoted J. Sperling Reich, "Primate Scream, Director Tim Burton Monkeys Around with Planet of the Apes," Reel.com. www.reel.com/reel.asp?node=features/interviews/burton.

Chapter 5: Chocolate and Corpses

11. Ifilm, "Charlie and the Chocolate Factory Interview with Tim Burton," http://www.ifilm.com/ifilmdetail/2659411?htv=12.

12. Quoted in Robin Rowe, "'Bride' Stripped Bare," *The Editors Guild Magazine*, Vol. 26, No. 4, July/August 2005.

13. Quoted in Ethan Aames, "Tim Burton on 'The Corpse Bride,'" *Cinema Confidential*, September 15, 2005. http://cinecon.com/news.php?id=0509151

14. Quoted in Mark Salisbury, "'Charlie and the Chocolate Factory' Set Visit," *Time Out London*, July 19, 2005. www.timeout.com/film/news/533.html.

GLOSSARY

animation: Filming a sequence of drawings or models that are only slightly different from frame to frame so that they appear to move and change when the frames are shown at a rapid rate.

apprentice: Somebody who learns a skill or trade by working for a person experienced in that field.

computer-generated image (CGI): A picture created on a computer using special imaging software.

conceptual artist: A person who uses art to convey an idea or concept.

director: Someone who supervises the actors and crew in the production of a show. The director usually oversees casting, lighting, music, sets, and most other elements of the production.

frame: An individual picture in a strip of many pictures that make up the movie film.

producer: Someone who finds financing for and supervises the making of a movie or stage production.

rights: The legal authority to produce a work such as a book or movie.

score: The music that has been composed for a movie or theater production.

screenplay: The script for a movie, including dialogue, directions for actors, and descriptions of sets.

sets: Artificially created environments used for filming scenes in a movie.

soundstages: Large indoor spaces where elaborate sets can be constructed for the purpose of filming movies.

stop-motion: An animation technique in which objects are filmed frame-by-frame and altered slightly between each frame.

storyboard: A sequence of drawings representing the shots planned for a film or television production.

suburb: A residential district located on the edge of a city or large town.

FOR FURTHER EXPLORATION

Books

Jane Brigham, *Johnny Depp*. Chicago, IL: Raintree, 2005. This biography of Johnny Depp includes information about his work with Tim Burton.

Tim Burton, *The Melancholy Death of Oyster Boy and Other Stories*. New York: William Morrow, 1997. Burton's somewhat disturbing book of short poems and illustrations featuring misshapen characters with sad stories.

Tim Burton, *Tim Burton's The Nightmare Before Christmas*. New York: Hyperion, 1997. Written in rhyming verse, this is the picture book version of the movie.

Tim Burton, *Tim Burton's The Nightmare Before Christmas (Manga)*. New York: Disney, 2005. This book tells the story in the Japanese Manga comic format.

Tim Burton and Mark Salisbury, *Tim Burton's Corpse Bride: An Invitation to the Wedding*. New York: New Market, 2005. This highly illustrated book discusses the making of *The Corpse Bride*. It includes drawings by Burton, storyboards, and lyrics to musical numbers in the film.

Roald Dahl, *Charlie and the Chocolate Factory*. New York: Puffin, 2005, 1964. The original book that the movie was based on. The 2005 edition features a picture from the movie on the cover.

Jake Hamilton, *Special Effects in Television and Movies*. New York: Dorling Kindersley, 1998. This colorful and informative book describes how many common special effects are created. The book includes many techniques used by Burton, including robotics, computer-generated images, and stop-motion animation. There is also a section about the history of special effects in the movies.

Damon J. Reinagle, *Draw Monsters: A Step-by-Step Guide.* Columbus, NC: Peel Productions, 2005. This book teaches kids how to draw all kinds of monsters.

Web Sites

Charlie and the Chocolate Factory (http://chocolatefactory movie.warnerbros.com). This is Warner Brothers' official site for the movie.

The Corpse Bride (http://corpsebridemovie.warnerbros.com). This is Warner Brothers' official site for the movie.

Halloween Town (http://halloweentown.org). This site offers a wealth of information about the movie *The Nightmare Before Christmas.* It includes the original Tim Burton poem that the movie was based on, as well as a link to the transcript of the movie.

Internet Movie Database: Tim Burton (http://www.imdb.com/name/nm0000318). This section of the database has a lot of information about Burton and his movies.

Tim Burton Collective (http://www.timburtoncollective.com). This is the most complete site on Tim Burton on the Web. There are articles, biographies, samples of his work, pictures, and even episodes of a cartoon Burton wrote called Stain Boy.

INDEX

Picture Credits

Cover: © Time-Life Pictures/Getty Images

© Alan Levenson/CORBIS, 17

© Close Murray/SYGMA/CORBIS, 31

© Frederick Lewis/Hulton Archive/Getty Images, 32

Geffen/Warner Bros./The Kobal Collection, 28

© Lloyd Gerald, 10

Maury Aaseng, 18

© Nicolas Guerin/Azimuts Productions/CORBIS, 7, 53

© Nancy Ostertag/Getty Images, 25

© Pierre Verdy/AFP/Getty Images, 47

© Sunset Boulevard/SYGMA/CORBIS, 12

© SYGMA/CORBIS, 38, 43

© Terry O'Neill/Hulton Archive/Getty Images, 29

© Time-Life Pictures/Getty Images, 23

Touchstone/The Kobal Collection, 40

Touchstone/Tim Burton/Di Novi/The Kobal Collection, 39

20th Century Fox/The Kobal Collection, 20, 34

20th Century Fox Television/The Kobal Collection, 35

Universal/The Kobal Collection, 11, 14

Warner Bros./The Kobal Collection, 8, 24, 42, 48

© Warner Bros./ ZUMA/CORBIS, 49, 52

Wolper/Warner Bros./The Kobal Collection, 51

ABOUT THE AUTHOR

Rachel Lynette has written a dozen other books for KidHaven Press as well as many articles on children and family life. Rachel's favorite Tim Burton movies are *Charlie and the Chocolate Factory* and *Frankenweenie*. Rachel lives in the Seattle area where she teaches science to children of all ages. When she is not writing or teaching, she enjoys spending time with her family and friends, traveling, reading, drawing, and in-line skating.